I0491705

# UNMASKING AMERICA

## A NATION'S CRY TO RACISM

### ANTHONY E. FISHER

© Copyright 2020 Anthony E. Fisher - All rights reserved.

This book is geared towards providing exact and reliable information in regards to the topic and issue covered. The publication is sold with the idea that the publisher is not required to render accounting, officially permitted, or otherwise, qualified services. If advice is necessary, legal or professional, a practiced individual in the profession should be ordered.

- From a Declaration of Principles which was accepted and approved equally by a Committee of the American Bar Association and a Committee of Publishers and Associations.

In no way is it legal to reproduce, duplicate, or transmit any part of this document in either electronic means or in printed format. Recording of this publication is strictly prohibited and any storage of this document is not allowed unless with written permission from the publisher. All rights reserved.

The information provided herein is stated to be truthful and consistent, in that any liability, in terms of inattention or otherwise, by any usage or abuse of any policies, processes, or directions contained within is the solitary and utter responsibility of the recipient reader. Under no circumstances will any legal responsibility or blame be held against the publisher for any reparation, damages, or monetary loss due to the information herein, either directly or indirectly.

Respective authors own all copyrights not held by the publisher.

The information herein is offered for informational purposes solely, and is universal as so. The presentation of the information is without contract or any type of guarantee assurance.

The trademarks that are used are without any consent, and the publication of the trademark is without permission or backing by the trademark owner. All trademarks and brands within this book are for clarifying purposes only and are the owned by the owners themselves, not affiliated with this document.

# TABLE OF CONTENTS

# INTRODUCTION

We are in a season of pandemics, having to deal with one global eruption after the other. While one was caused by an outsider, a small organism that cannot be seen with the naked eyes, yet capable of causing disasters of unimaginable magnitude, the others are caused by habits and attitudes inherent to us. It is a tale of every man for himself. We either fight for what is right or allow ourselves to be trodden upon, like threadbare carpets that nobody wants.

The streets are hot and unsafe with peaceful protests that have turned violent. But for once, cogent issues that appeared to have been swept under the carpet are finally getting addressed, and who knows, maybe become laid to rest. The year 2020 surely came with its script and agenda, and we are the actors, prepared to see the end of the movie; one that seems to be unending.

We started on an unstable note with the emergence of a new virus that has continued to defy cure and preventive measures set up by the best of the brains. Many countries are working-hand-in-hand to battle this common enemy, and for a moment, the race to become the renowned world power appears to take the backseat.

However, while we seek to eliminate a strange virus that appears to be on a mission against the entire human race, we have left a systemic flaw and an innate virus that can do worse and irreparable damage than the novel coronavirus. While several countries are setting up stringent measures to reopen to prevent a collapse of economies, we have ignored a fundamental issue that can wipe away all we have built for many years in a single move because we can't tolerate one another. That issue called racism.

So what is racism? Racism is defined as the belief that groups of humans possesses different behavior traits corresponding to physical appearance and can be divided based on the superiority of one race over another. It may also mean, prejudice, discrimination or antagonism directed against other people because they are of a different race or ethnicity.

In short, racism, a biting and unyielding virus, is the cankerworm that has shaken the entire world to the very roots. Over time, it has separated us, led to violence, caused untold death tolls, hardships, and worse of all, led to a crippling fear that can, in turn, lead to worse consequences if not properly dealt with. Displacing the preexisting COVID-19, racism came to the forefront to effectively take over the position of COVID-19, pushing it to the back.

No one thought about social distancing in the fight for the right justice and equality of all races. No one remembered that there was a need to wash hands, use masks, and practice protecting procedures when the chant of "Black Lives matter" filled the air. And yes, black lives do matter.

We are all humans, with a right to life and fair treatment regardless of the differences in our colors. Our colors are works of arts that science has delved into and linked to varying compositions of the melanin pigment. The pigmentation does not define us. It does not dictate how we act or react, and definitely, it should not be the yardstick to measure who gets fair treatment and who does not.

Should racism be allowed to go unchecked? Should people get their rights trampled upon because they are from a colored minority group? The resounding answer is no. It can't and won't be allowed. This pandemic should be expunged from our midst. If all hands can go on deck to combat COVID-19, then, it is time for us to also come together again to clean and rid our systems of RACISM. Let us say no to racism and everything attached to it. Black lives are equal to any other race and black lives also matter . We are getting rid of the pandemic in a pandemic, and there is no backing down this time. People of color are simply tired of the inequality that takes place on America's soil.

This country, America the land of liberty, the land of the free, has been terrorizing the black communities for far too long.. One of the most horrible and devastating day in history was in May 1985, the Philadelphia police dropped a bomb on a West Philly neighborhood, specifically on the house of a Black liberation group called MOVE, killing 11 people, including 5 children, destroying 61 homes and leaving 250 people homeless? The Move was an organization, a black liberation group, led and founded by John Africa (born Vincent Leaphart) who taught the MOVE members about corruption in the american system. They were advocates for justice and believed that their lives should be treated as equally important as their counterparts.

On the day of the bombing, the police were sent to the MOVE house to execute arrest warrants for several members. When those inside the house refused to respond, the authorities decided to take extreme measures. They somehow justified the use of military grade weapons, despite their knowledge of children on the premises.

500 police officers shot 10,000 rounds of ammo with automatic weapons at the house. The police commissioner then ordered to bomb the house, with a helicopter dropping a satchel bomb, a demolition device typically used in combat, onto the roof. After detonation, officials let the fire spread throughout the neighborhood. The fire-fighters were told not to fight the fire by the police commissioner named Gregore J.Sambor.

Despite this event being the only account of an aerial US bombing, of US citizens on US soil no one was ever prosecuted. The evil act of bombing of this community was indeed an act of systemic racism.Today, other nationalities are joining the people of color and crying out and standing in solidarity because enough is enough!

# CHAPTER 1

# A TRIP DOWN MEMORY LANE

———○———

America was a country born by the coming-together of many migrants, especially those leaving Europe for a greener Pasture and in search of freedom from strict religious rules. So, if there is any land owned by no one and free for all, it is America. A land boosted by its numerous channels of natural resources and diverse population united by landmass, it was a land coveted and loved by many. Many in the present days still dream of walking its streets of gold. Under one umbrella, the people prospered, and it was the ideal location for the American Dream to spring up and prosper.

Championed by Benjamin Franklin, a man with less than adequate formal education, the American Dream got birthed and defined. On July 4, 1976, noblemen of the Second Continental Congress sat down to discuss and adopt the Declaration of Independence Pronouncement, strong backing for the birth of the must-have American Dream. While the exact date of individual signing remains a debate among many, it is inconsequential as the Declaration became an official statement on July 4.

"We hold these truths to be self-evident, that all men are created equal, that they are endowed by their Creator with certain unalienable Rights, that among these are Life, Liberty and the pursuit of Happiness." These lines sealed a fate that was yet set for a tortuous journey.

With fifty-six (56) signatures, America was free well for everybody to draw from, or so it seemed. In this Declaration, a levelled ground became available to every man, regardless of race, color, and ethnicity. As long as you were willing to pay the price of hard work, America was the place to stay. The influence of the Declaration was strong, especially as many other countries adopted similar strategies and documents.

However, the document had little power in the minds of the people it was intended for. It was not a piece that interested many. The fun-fare of gaining independence from Great Britain clouded the Declaration that announced it. Rather, the people gave more importance to another- the Declaration of Rights.

If these statements were wrong about those lived in those periods, then, the current happenings give strong backing to it. However, the earlier generations and founding fathers can't be absolved of any wrongdoing concerning ill-treatment and despicable acts against blacks and other minority groups as well. The Declaration of Independence was what it was; a piece of an official document that heralded America as a free nation but held no power over its people. It was only an idea as truths exist in the minds of people. Their perception of what is the truth drives their actions, and the Declaration of Independence was anything but that, remaining relevant on official papers but holding no water with the people. Hence, the notion of truth has always been a matter of debate and question.

As inconsequential as the document was to its intended people, it championed a lot of reactions from others who saw a golden opportunity too good to be missed, resulting in the pursuit of the American Dream. People of color of various racial backgrounds milled to the land flowing with milk, honey, and sweet promises of a better life. However, the "freedom for all" paraded by the Declaration was perhaps, only a mirage. That is, regardless of what was written, the intent communicated by the Declaration of Independence missed its target, giving room to immigrants after only they have become part of the fold. However, this inclusion was not generally accepted. Benjamin Franklin dedicated most of his life to ensuring that equality was a norm in a country with a less-than glorious history of the promotion of commerce centered on slavery, but the people never forget.

Geared by a desire to strike out by himself after serving President Grover Cleveland, in addition to the land rush that lasted between 1889 and 1891, O. W. Gurley, a young entrepreneur vast in land purchase and sales set his eyes on Oklahoma. The wealthy African American completed his move in 1906 by moving down to Tulsa in Oklahoma with land measuring 40 acres to his name, only to be sold to people of color. It was a great achievement at a time when it was impossible to own properties and almost anything as a black. In addition to his large expanse of land, Gurley boasted of a rooming house which later became a popular destination for many migrating African-America seeking succor and sense of belonging among their own, and three two-storeys and five buildings enable for residential capacity. He also owned a farm of about eighty acres (80 acres) in Rogers County. He built and founded the Vernon AME Church.

Following on the heels of O.W. Gurley, J.B. Stradford, another equally enterprising African- American set his eyes on Tulsa in 1899. He had an idea that served as a foundation for O.W. Gurley and other black enthusiasts. However, his vision was on a large scale with the belief that Africa-American stood a great chance, if not a better one, at economic success with combined resources and support for each other's businesses. As a result, he invested in land procurement, buying large parcels of land covering a significant expanse in Northeastern Tulsa. These lands were later divided and sold to only blacks for settlement and business. Not resting on his oars, Stradford expanded his business outreach by constructing, operating, and owning the Stradford Hotel which catered to only blacks. As a result, people of color could enjoy the same amenities and facilities that were only reserved for whites in the downtown hotels. Stradford Hotel was the largest ever black-owned hotel in the United States of America.

In 1907, on the 18th December, the Senate Bill One was approved by Oklahoma's first Legislature, reinforcing the hold of racism and discrimination in a land that once claimed that all lives were equal. Championed a majorly racist congregation of noblemen, the Bill read thus; "every railway company, urban or suburban car company, streetcar or interurban car or railway company ... shall provide separate coaches or compartments as hereinafter provided for the accommodation of the white and negro races, which separate coaches or cars shall be equal in all points of comfort and convenience."

In some parts of the bill, railway companies were compelled to provide depots with clearly identified waiting rooms and services ordered according to the status of each race. Going further, penalty fees were levied against offenders, starting from one hundred to one thousand dollars ($100-$1000) for companies that defied the order and five to twenty-five dollars ($5- $25) for persons who failed to comply in any way. In other words, the legislation demanded the provision of separate and distinct public transportation facilities, education, consideration, rights, places, and other situations for blacks. They upheld the white-supremacy idea and fueled the ever-burning embers of racism. Railroad officials were also fully empowered by the Bill to refuse to provide service or remove offenders. As expected, this Bill did not sit with many blacks, resulting in several riots, some violent, in the black communities.

With ever rising and harsh racial discrimination in Oklahoma and many other parts of America, many African Americans turned to Greenwood, Tulsa for succor. Mississippi was well-known for high levels of racism, slavery, and discrimination, forcing many to flee to the greener pasture Tulsa represented. Finally, the dreams of Stradford and Gurley became established. This was also partly driven by the rush and prospects of the oil and mining industries. Nevertheless, the extreme racial discrimination significantly contributed to the high influx of African Americans to Greenwood, resulting in fast-paced development that further irked the surrounding and less-fortunate white community.

Greenwood, Tulsa, later became dubbed the "Black Wall Street" in recognition of its commercial success, economic prowess, affluence, and influence among the African American settlements in America. Setting an unprecedented pace, the average income far outweighed what is considered the minimum wage in today's financial sector. Records have it that six black families boasted of owning private planes in a state where only two airports existed. The success of Black Wall Street was stimulated by the enclosed method of commerce, ensuring that the dollar traded well among its members before leaving the community, as high as thirty-six to hundred times (36 to 100).

By 1913, the African American community boasted of Buck Colbert Franklin's Law Office, a doctor's place owned by A.C. Jackson, the Vernon AME church, The Williams Dreamland Theater, Baptist worship centers, the Ricketts Restaurant, Dunbar and Booker T. Washington

Schools, a host of grocery stores, cafes, salons, and eye-popping commercial centers. Restricted by the Second Bill One, many African Americans had no choice but to turn to Greenwood for business pursuits and transactions. The community enjoyed an upper-class lifestyle and luxury that was a thorn in the flesh of their larger white-dominated neighbors.

However, the fall of Black Wall Street was imminent, along with the fame and prosperity accrued by prominent members such as O.W. Gurley. In 1921, approximately ninety-nine years (99 years) ago, the Black Wall Street fell to a racism-fuelled massacre by its white neighbors who had been silently irked by the prosperity of the former in a land considered theirs. In their opinion, the blacks were meant to be subservient and take second-class positions to them. Greenwood was an aberration and an affront to what was meant to be the standard.

Sketchy details about the happenings of that day exist, but for a fact, the jealous white neighbors rode on the wings of racism and envy to bring down a deck of cards that was Black Wall Street. The underlying cause of the riot that broke out that day is also partly attributed to a racially instigated report released by the *Tulsa Tribune*, a newspaper company, on the 31st May, of 1921. In that issue, an African American by the name Dick Rowland was accused of trying to force himself on Sarah Page, a white woman who happened to be in an elevator with him in the Drexel building on that unfortunate day. The 19-year old shoe shiner had no opportunity to defend himself while the 17-year old Sara Page did not press charges against him. However, the inflamed incidence was the right opportunity for the white neighbors of Greenwood to act on a simmering and long-standing boiling pot of hatred. Several reports hold that hateful and racially discriminating letters had been sent to prominent members and businesses of Greenwood before the opportunity for the massacre opened up.

At the end of the massive two-days hateful destruction of Greenwood, about three hundred (300) people had lost their lives, eight hundred (800) were fatally injured, and thirty-five (35) city blocks laid in ruins after being set ablaze. About nine thousand (9000) African Americans also lost their homes in that dark and troubling incidence.

The systemic racism was evident even amid the black inferno that consumed Greenwood. Not only were the blacks outnumbered by the racial white neighbors, but several African Americans were also locked up while not a single white arrest was made even though witnesses reported several lootings and burning were carried out by them. The police force took a racial stand, disregarding necessary operational protocols and increasing the police strength with enraged whites armed with guns provided by them.

As if that wasn't enough, the Government, Media and News Outlets significantly contributed and supported the racial rot in the system. Several lopsided versions of the true cause and nature of the incidence were released, painting the African Americans in the most despicable manner and justifying the rationale that they needed to be shown their place in the community. The 'lawless blacks' were also accused of starting the riot. The Government was also accused of not helping out with aids to rebuild Greenwood and recoup losses suffered by the African American community even though it promised to do so. This matter was revisited in 1997 leading to a formation of a committee charged with investigating the possibility of compensating descendants of victims of the massacre. A positive recommendation was released after four years (4 years) in 2001 for the descendants of the affected to receive full reparations. In 2010, memorials in honour of the sufferers of the 1921 Greenwood massacre were created after many petitions, lobbying, and publications were made.

Although many white neighbors promised to help out, those promises were never fulfilled. Instead, many saw it as an opportunity to loot and make massive wealth from the despondent state of the impoverished African Americans. They offered to buy their lands at ridiculous prices, compelling a lot of blacks to give up at measly prices to meet up with financial obligations and survival. Indeed, all tables were turned against the most successful and advanced black community. All legal suits made against the city became overturned by the Government, leaving the people powerless and helpless. Nevertheless, an attempt at rebuilding was made, and in the year 1922, a year after the massacre, approximately eighty (80) African American-owned businesses had started operations again in the area. However, the area never achieved its lost former prominence and affluence.

The sad story not only shows that racism existed long before now, but it also gives support to the fact that it is deeply ingrained in the system at all fronts, beginning from the Government, the Police Force, and the people. The attempt to cover up the true nature of the massacre and then watering it down the history lane exposes a miserable attempt of America at pretending that racism is not second nature to many of her citizens. Critically examining American capitalism, a segment of white elites is always ensured to remain in power to influence the American socioeconomic system to maintain white supremacy.

# CHAPTER 2

# THE TRIGGER

On the 25th of May 2020, a video went viral on the internet. In it, an unarmed black man with no evidence of having resisted arrest was pinned to the ground by a White man in Police uniform. The Police Officer held the man, restricting his movements and access to fresh air by kneeling on his neck despite the latter's plea for some air because of his inability to breathe. The shout of "I can't breathe" repeatedly resonated from the helpless man throughout the short video recording, but they fell on deaf ears. A picture of helplessness and hopelessness was created in that short clip, characterized by a depth of evil and relentless wickedness that can be meted out during the abuse of power and authority fueled by racism.

The police officer remained unperturbed and unabated in his brutal dealings while his colleagues warded off interferences and interventions from the persons recording the video. The assaulted man was George Floyd, a forty-six-year-old (46 years) African American, and the unfortunate incidence led to his demise. His lifeless body got loaded onto a stretcher at the tail end of the video. Before the end of the day, the streets were filled with protesters decrying the animalistic treatment meted out to George Floyd. Was the use of a counterfeit twenty-dollar ($20) note enough to claim the life of the forty-six (46) years old man? The question is, was it about Floyd, or did he serve as the trigger to a loaded gun ready to go off any second? How many Georges will have to lay their lives down like lambs to ensure that the system gets wiped out and racism is a forgotten issue in the land?

Unfortunate it was, but the truth is that the issue was beyond George Floyd and his murder. George Floyd and the circumstances surrounding his death represented the daily life of a typical African American, the fear, and the undeserved systemic injustice and hate faced from time to time. George served as the trigger and focus that brought a new wave of revolution, one in which every man must stand up for himself or remain silent forevermore. However, this time around, silence is not golden.

A quick reexamination of history shows that Police brutality against people of color, particularly blacks, did not just begin. It is so much ingrained in the society that it has become a norm, with many living in fear and doing everything possible to stay out of trouble. While some of the killings and brutality meted out to African Americans were of high profiles, drawing reactions and sometimes violent protests from members of the black communities, many were not, and most of these killings got swept under the carpet. About ninety-nine per cent (99 %) of these unjust killings did not result in charges against the offending police officers.

A study to map out police violence revealed some interesting but simultaneously disturbing facts. Although blacks were rated to be 1.3 times more likely to be unarmed during an arrest compared to Hispanics and Whites, they were 3 times more likely to be killed by the police. The report further showed that killings did not occur only on twenty-seven days in 2019. That's not even up to a month! In the same study, it was revealed that the residential locations determined the rate of murder, with police killing about 6 times higher in Oklahoma than Georgia. Lastly, the rate of police killings was not determined by the level of crimes and violence. There was no correlation between the two occurrences. Without being armed and not posing any immediate danger, what informs the pulling of the trigger? The only answer to that question is hatred. Hatred toward someone who you see as inferior to you does not give you consent to pull any triggers!

Even after the death of George Floyd, police brutality continued to rise. Not even a month after the fatal killing of Mr. Floyd, another unarmed Black male was fatally killed by the Atlanta Police Department (APD) in a public parking lot. His name was Rayshard Brooks. A 27 year old African-American whose life was taken by the brutality of a white racist police officer. It triggered unrest and new waves of protest around the country and the world. Mr. Brooks did not deserve to have his life taken by the hands of racist officers in uniform. He did not deserve to leave this earth in such an undignified manner.

He was shot multiple times in his back while running away from these officers. He feared for his life. To add insult to this tradegy, after fatally killing this unarmed black man, the officer kicked the victim as he lay bleeding and placed his foot on the victim's shoulder, provided no medical attention and stated, "I got him." Because of the civil unrest in the city, this officer, Garrett Rolfe, faces eleven charges including murder and aggravated assault. This also led to many APD officers stepping down from their positions. Perhaps the guilt is too overwhelming. Perhaps the bad cops are purging themselves out of the system in FEAR of what they have done wrong in their own past. Hopefully,

America is left with the ones who actually took the oath "protect and serve" seriously and with the right intentions. Brooks had simply feel asleep in his car.

American police brutality and discrimination against African Americans has its roots deeply ingrained in a long history of slavery and a racially biased legal system that provides not only the necessary backing but also a form of protection that encourages such dastardly acts.

About four hundred (400) years back, as far back as the 1700s, the use of Slave Patrols was a welcomed and encouraged necessity as the act of slavery (a condition in which a human being can own a fellow human being against their will) was well-established back in those days. An enslaved person was controlled by his master, who provided where he lived and worked. A person could become enslaved from the time of their capture, purchase or birth.

Slavery existed in many societies and was once legal in most societies in the past but now it is abolished.

In 1789-1865, the blacks were enslaved by the whites. Slavery in the U.S was a legal institution of human chattel enslavement, primarily of natives Africans and African Americans. Slavery existed in the United States of America from the beginning of the nation until the enactment of the Thirteenth Amendment in 1865.

Before the enaction of the Thirteenth Amendment in 1865, the whites were the master of the blacks. A black enslaved individual was treated as property and could be bought or sold or given away at any time by his master.

Slave codes were created and are known as the subset of laws regarding slavery and enslaved people, specifically concerning the Atlantics slave trade and chattel slavery in the Americas. The slave codes were concerned with the rights and duties of free people in regarding on how to enslave another individual.

The Slave code varied from one colony to another and the slave code was being constantly altered to adapt to new needs. Slave codes prohibited a slave from testifying against his white master, they couldn't own property and they could not leave their owner premises without permission. Even when attacked by a white person, they could not strike back, they were prohibited from owning firearms, they were not allowed to marry and they were not permitted to be taught to read or write.

These slave codes were expected to be followed by the slaves and failure to do so would result in punishment.

Slaves (often blacks) were considered less human, more commonly classed as animals and treated as such. Therefore, stringent measures unbefitting to any human were mostly enforced and used on them. Hard whipping and imprisonment were commonly used. Sadly, some enslaved people who committed violence against whites were eliminated (killed). The slave patrols constituted of white volunteers who were empowered and armed to forcefully return escaped slaves to their masters. Also, they were charged with using brutality and unconventional means such as lynching to stop slave-staged protests. They had access to anyone's house regardless of the race and a standby search warrant to fish out escape slaves.

During the enslavement period of Africans in America, the Meritorious Manumission Act of 1710 was enacted in Virginia. It was the legal act of releasing slaves for "good deeds." This freedom could be granted to a slave for rescuing the life of a White master, creating an invention that the slavemaster could benefit or profit from, or the most commonly used word, "snitching" on a slave who planned a revolt or decided to run away for their freedom. This law that was enacted was a law that has affected blacks to this day.

It's critical that the black family understands how big of an impact this law had on not just our community but on the psyche as well. If you consider the 200-plus slave revolts that were attempted from the year 1710 to approximately the late 1800's, most of the revolts were unsuccessful for one main reason. A slave who was scared or felt they wanted a better seat in the Master's house or a better position with his Master would tell on any slave revolt they knew was going to be forming. Even if they didn't have a lot of information they used that tactic to free themselves. This was the tactic that ran rampant in the black community at the time and this was one of the many tactics that the dominant white society used to create separation and mistrust within the African American community.

In the Eighteenth Century, the government of the United States, especially in the American South started to make requirements regulating the liberation of slaves and their role in society. Within, African American and Native American slaves could gain their freedom through manumission. However, they could not obtain white settlers as indentured servants in the cause of their freedom. But they could obtain their own freedom Native Americans or African Americans as slaves.

In the nineteenth century, manumission was seen as one of the appropriate methods to control the African American population in the southern United States. Southern leaders were feeling insecure that freed slaves coupled with support from abolitionists and religious organizations would result in more numerous and stronger slave revolts in the future. The Southern United States decided to control the process of manumission through the court system.

In 1830, North Carolina manumission cases were moved from the county courts to a more restrictive superior court. Slave masters had to submit a written petition to the superior court if he is willing to free a slave through manumission. Also, he had to publish a notice in the newspaper stating his aim of giving his slave freedom through manumission six weeks before the act of liberation. The Religious bodies tried to find a way around the courts imploring them to use manumission for slave freedom. The higher state courts ruled that manumission could not violate the state laws concerning the African American slave society. State supreme courts started to rule in favor of the restrictive slave laws and manumission for slave freedom was becoming small in number and unsuccessful.

The slaves that gained their freedom through manumission in the Southern United States are expected to leave the state once a manumission petition was granted. In North Carolina, a freed slave had within ninety days to leave the state and failure to do that, he will be enslaved back and if the freeman returns to the state, he could be arrested or sold back into slavery.

Before the United States Civil War, the manumission rate reduced drastically throughout the South. This is due to the fear of slave rebellions and economic development generated by the use of enslaved people for the production and harvest of cash crops. As a result of fear of rebellions and crashes in economic prosperity, the white masters were not willing to free their slaves with manumission.

Also, the freed African American slaves lost many of the civil liberties that they had once enjoyed during the colonial government period. The freed African American slaves were now forced to register with the county superior courts in order for their movements to be monitored and tracked within the white community.

In 1860, most southern states had eliminated all legislation that supported any form of emancipation including manumission. With this, the leadership of white society became assured that the African American Society, whether free or slave was within their sight, control, and supervision.

It's important to understand that establishing an invisible hierarchy based on Good Deeds for people without a hope for identity was pretty much a recipe for disaster. It's also important to note that the lingering effects of this can still be found amongst the minority black community today. This is the gist of the meritorious manumission.

At the beginning of the 19th Century, the Centralized Municipal Police Departments sprang up in place of the slave patrols as organized bodies, but the modus operandi was still similar to those of the slave patrols. The recruits were untrained, mostly white males, and responded to disorderliness rather than crimes. Part of their job was to make sure that the dangerous underclass (primarily African Americans, the poor, and the immigrants) remained subdued and under control. All these served as the foundation for the modern-day police brutality. In cases where African Americans were recruited into the Force, they were deployed to the black communities and heavily discriminated against by the greater number of white colleagues.

The Civil War brought a formal end to slavery after the ratification of the 13th Amendment, but it's quite impossible to wash off a leopard's spots from its skin. The African Americans were still a long way away from the perceived rest from discrimination and racial bias. The Black Codes sprang up in place of the slavery conditions. These were attempts of the Government and the white communities to ensure that African Americans remained subdued to them. It was difficult to totally relish the control they had enjoyed for many years. The police departments were entrusted with the duty of ensuring that the people complied with these laws, empowering and encouraging brutality against the people of colors.

Through the ratification of the 14th Amendment in 1868, providing equal protection to everyone regardless of the race, many expected respites from the now illegal Black Codes, but those were mere fantasies of an imaginative heart. The Jim Crow Laws sprang up to speedily take the place of the Black Codes. These were harsh, legal conditions that enforced the use of separate public facilities by the black minority. Denial of blacks' civil rights such as the right to vote and be voted for, access to education, and freedom reigned during the eighty years Jim Crow Laws were enforced on the people. Anyone who stepped out of line was made subject to police brutality.

Bias also characterized the legal systems of those times as blacks suffered longer sentences with harsher pronouncements. Most times, many of them did not live long enough to fulfill the lengthy sentences dished out to them. The police were also guilty of siding and aiding the white communities during mob fights and protests. Lack of accountability on the side of the law enforcers and failure to charge evil perpetrators as expected all encouraged white supremacy ideas. The lynching of African Americans was a common occurrence which often resulted in more violent protests and increased black arrests. In most cases, whites walked away scot-free.

The Jim Crow Laws were finally and officially abolished with the enactment of the Fair Housing Act of 1968, but subsequent events showed that the depth of systemic racism and police brutality ran deep and were a long way from being over. A 2018 study reported by *The Washington Post* revealed that despite only making up about twelve per cent of the country, African Americans accounted for twenty-three per cent of those killed by the Police.

# CHAPTER 3

# SCOT FREE

In 1991, a young twenty-five-year-old (25 years) Rodney King was beaten and molested by four white police officers for driving under the influence and trying to resist arrest. While the young man might have been guilty of the offence, the force and following punishment were unjustified. The more than 50-baton strokes dealt on the young man left him with permanent brain damage and other numerous health issues. It was the beginning of constant doctors' visit for the young man. Unbelievably, the four officers seen in the video, filmed and released by a passer-by, were acquitted and released, cementing the lack of accountability and the presence of racial injustice in the police force. The incidence and acquittal of the officers led to violent protests spanning over six days. During this time, about six thousand arrests were made and over fifty people got killed. The numbers of those who sustained fatal injuries ran into thousands.

Eight years later, the death of twenty-three years old Amadou Diallo was all over the news. The young man was gunned down by men of the force in plain clothes close to his house on the suspicion that he had a gun. The four men fired a total of forty-one (41) shots into the unarmed man who only made the mistake of reaching for his wallet at that time. Many protesters took to the streets to not only condemn the act but also decry the acquittal of the four men involved in the action that can be classified as second-degree murder. While most of the protests were peaceful, the reaction of the police officers showed that they were prepared and ready to take on the worst situation.

The unfortunate death of Amadou Diallo led to disbanding of the Street Crimes Unit of NYPD who had been accused several times of high racial discrimination against African Americans and Hispanics in the discharge of their duties. The four police officers belonged to the Street Crimes Unit.

In 2006, five police officers fired a total of fifty-one (51) shots into three young men namely Sean Bell, Joseph Guzman, and Trent Benefield. The twenty-three-year-old Sean Bell who was set to walk down the aisle in few hours lost his life in the process, while his other two friends were fatally wounded. Going further in a show of sheer brutality and gloating, the injured men were shackled to their beds in the hospital during treatment. This act led to an outcry by the masses. Only three of the officers were charged, but they eventually got off the hook, leading to their acquittal. Unwilling to succumb to the expectation of violent protests, peaceful rallies were held in honor of the men, with African Americans demanding justice and righting of the lopsided judicial system.

Another young African American saw the life snuffed out of him in 2011. His name was Anthony Lamar Smith. The officer who committed the dastardly act claimed that he suspected Smith of dealing in drugs and shot at him after the latter tried escaping from him. However, he was later charged in 2016 after a video clip showed him saying some very explicit language that he was "going to kill this mother…..". However, the officer walked away free again in 2017 after he was acquitted of his offences. He defended his actions by claiming that he saw Smith with a gun. Being armed and considered dangerous was enough to allow him to engage in the shooting.

However, several days of protests erupted after the Court's ruling, some of which had mild elements of violence. The police responded by turning up in riot gears, used rubber bullets, and arrested several persons. Later, the St. Louis police paid the family of the deceased a total of one million, four hundred dollars ($1.4 m) in 2013 and 2019 for wrongful death and planting of the said weapon in the deceased's car by the offending officer. Nevertheless, the officer was never brought to book.

Police brutality took an ugly turn for worse in 2014 with the death of the forty-three years old Eric Garner. Garner's case was a blatant display of sheer wickedness and disregard for life with a close resemblance to what happened to George Floyd. After accusing Garner of peddling untaxed cigarettes, the undercover police agent held the deceased in a forbidden chokehold. The recording showed the suspect pleading several times that he could not breathe, but the officer was unyielding and relentless. A few hours later, Garner was confirmed unresponsive and dead. The act and the decision of the Grand Jury to acquit the police officer resulted in a peaceful protest that spanned over several days.

Justice was not served until five years later, resulting in a dismissal of the officer in 2019 when the Civilian Complaint Review Board (CCRB) started a fresh trial against the offender. Nevertheless, it is important to mention that both Staten Island Grand Jury and federal prosecutors refused to charge the officer involved in the shooting. Recently, on the 8th of June 2020, many members of the New York Assembly voted to criminalize the utilization of chokeholds by the police, a long-overdue process.

Barely a month after the brutal killing of Garner, another police officer killed Michael Brown by firing twelve (12) shots into the young man just at his prime. At eighteen years, Brown got his life ended by police brutality after a convenience store's camera picked him up shoplifting cigars. Although guilty of the act, Brown was unarmed, and no documents ever showed him resisting arrest. Daren Wilson, the man who had committed the act, was never indicted. Still reeling from the recent incidence of Garner's murder, Brown's death and the Jury's stand did not sit well with many people, resulting in several violent protests. The unreprimanded police force responded in the same way, using repressive methods as harsh as varieties of military weapons and tear gasses to stop the advancement of the protesters. They got the weapons as a result of the Department of Defense's 1033 program set up to make such military gadgets available to law enforcements functioning at the local level.

As a result, the "Black Lives Matter" movement became intense, rejecting the kind of systemic bias prevalent in institutionalized authorities and the judicial system. The movement had previously started as an online initiative in 2012 after the killing of Trayvon Martin. Also, the mantra, "Hands up, don't shoot," became generated. The launching of "Campaign Zero," an offshoot of "Black Lives Matter" began in 2015. It demanded the limited use of force and brutality by the police while discharging their duties.

Several interventions followed the death of Michael Brown. Under the administration of President Barack Obama, the first black American President, the Department of Defense's 1033 program became abolished, demilitarizing the police to an extent. However, the program was reestablished through an executive order under the administration of President Donald Trump in the year 2017.

A twelve-year-old, Tamir Rice suffered an unfortunate death in the hands of two officers in Cleveland shortly after Brown's killing. The excuse for the act was the assumption of arms possession by the child, who was not even in his teen years yet. What the officers assumed to be a fully loaded gun turned out to be a pellet gun. Both officers were not charged, but the incidence got Tim McGinty voted out in 2016 for calling the act "a perfect storm of human error." A peaceful march was staged to protest the death of Rice.

On the 12th of April 2015, after what seemed like a period of respite from public protests and high-profile police killings and brutality, Freddie Gray got arrested on the grounds of having a switchblade in his possession. On the way to the police station, Gray became subjected to the 'rough ride' routine practice. In the process, he suffered an extensive spinal cord injury after being jerked by the sudden application of brakes by the driver of the police van. Gray later succumbed to his injuries after an agonizing week in treatment.

A peaceful protest followed Gray's death, which became increasingly violent as he got laid to rest on April 27 of 2015. To disperse the protesters, the police used pepper spray and tear gas. More than two hundred protesters were arrested during the violent march. The then Baltimore Mayor, Stephanie Rawlings-Blake declared curfew while Governor Larry Hogan of Maryland declared a state of emergency. However, protests abated once the six police officers were charged. Nevertheless, none of these men ever served any term. Three of them got acquitted while charges against the remaining three were dropped. Fresh protests started again on the heels of these new developments; however, they were mostly peaceful. Gray's death signaled the beginning of a new movement- Baltimore's Social Activist Community.

On July 5th and 6th of July 2016, two black men got killed in different and unrelated events. Thirty-seven years old Alton Sterling was eliminated on the 5th of July when an anonymous call to the police reported him for peddling his CDs in front of a convenience store. The man was approached by two white police officers, but one pulled the trigger, killing Sterling on the spot after claiming that the later reached for his gun. The videos that surfaced later revealed the blatancy of the lie and excuse given by the officer. Sterling did not make any movement before his life was taken away from him.

In what had become an expected and predictable move of murder and protests, protesters took to the streets of Louisiana to condemn the act and to seek justice for the dead man. Although the protests were largely peaceful, the police came out to meet the people in full combatant mode, leading to several unlawful arrests. The officers were never brought to book even though the Department of Justice made a feeble attempt at civil rights investigation of the case. However, the officer who pulled the trigger was immediately dismissed from active service. The following day, Philando Castile was murdered in Minnesota.

The 6th of July brought fresh fears and despair to the people with the death of the school nutritionist in the presence of his girlfriend and her daughter. Castile got pulled over by officer Yanez, which he did without hassle. Asked to produce his driver's license and registration, Castile complied but also informed the officer of a gun in the glove compartment of the car, which happened to be where he kept his documents too. There was nothing illegal about that because he had the necessary license to carry one. Yanez rounded several shots into the man as he reached to get his documents. The video of the entire interaction was captured and released by the girlfriend on the internet. Nonetheless, the officer walked away scot-free in 2017.

Touched by the turn of events, many protesters, including children, teachers, and the Black Lives Matter movement decried the act of police brutality. The police, in turn, reacted with more violence and arrests. In response, the United States Department of Justice began a review of the St. Anthony police department in 2016. However, reports had it that all objectives were only drafted on paper and never followed through by actions. The then U.S President Barack Obama identified with Castile's death while also admitting the existence of police brutality. He termed it an "American issue," confirming the long-standing presence of systemic racial bias and discrimination ingrained in the justice system.

Lastly, we come back to the trigger. At a time when tensions are naturally high and people are distraught, the death of George Floyd is the ignition needed to offset the bag of gunpowder. In the video of almost nine minutes, Floyd begged for his life, to no success. The chauvinistic officer Chauvin displayed a plain disregard for life and extreme racism to the extent of murder without batting an eye. This time around, African Americans will not sit with their hands folded, while the lives of blacks are claimed like chickens. And perhaps, this time, the entire world is having the scales removed from their eyes.

# CHAPTER 4

# FIGHT FOR FREEDOM

There's a total disregard for African American lives sustained by a system that supports and encourages acts of white supremacy enacted by those meant to protect the people. Over time, lack of accountability and failure to indict offending officers have been the bedrocks of police brutality, furnishing the continuity of a system that seems to resist change.

The chants of mantras such as "Black Lives Matter," "Hands up, don't shoot," and other statements supporting the abolishment of racial discrimination and marginalization of the minority groups have been crystallized and taken a more solid turn over time. The death of George Floyd brought that, but much more than that, the people are strung out and need to find a lasting solution to racism and racial killings.

When there is no more an escape route or plan, the next thing is to choose between whether to fly or fight. For several years, the flight response was selected over fighting. For instance, after the unlawful and jealousy-driven destruction of the economic progress and homes of African Americans in Greenwood, Tulsa, and the failure of the Government to put necessary measures in place, many blacks were afraid to protest. They feared that protesting the unjust treatment was likely to cause a repeat of the incidence, a nightmare many of them wanted to leave behind. For those who stood up to fight by requesting some aids and suing the government, they soon found out that it was a lost cause.

Over time, for peace to reign and for the thuggery perception many had of African Americans to be erased, most killings had been peacefully protested but stopped as soon as things had the writings of getting out of hand. However, all of these measures and sacrifices seem to be ineffective. Instead, the brutality endured by the people in the hands of police got worse. An average black man and woman lived with fear, not knowing when all hell will break loose or if there is a certainty about the future. Why should people who only want the best for themselves and their children live in constant fear because of a color difference?

Now, the way forward is in fighting for a freedom that seems long overdue.

## "BLACK LIVES MATTER"

The "Black Lives Matter" movement and protests have been ongoing for sometime now, and it appears not to be easing up anytime soon. In contrast, the fire of solidarity and demand for basic rights and protection of lives, that should have been the norm, keeps increasing every day. For once, it appears that the people are demanding that they must be heard. Regardless of the extreme measures taken by the police to curtail these protests, the people are not ready to give up; at least, not on this one. The following reasons are factors fanning the glowing embers of this protest.

- **The existing tension of COVID-19:** The COVID-19 pandemic realities have brought unprecedented harsh conditions on everyone, but most especially the African American communities, leaving many on edge and probably swift to react than before. In February 2020, reports revealed that the rate of unemployment among African American was 5.8 %, almost twice of their white counterpart which was 3.1 %, and the overall national unemployment rate at 3.5 %. That was way before the COVID-19 pandemic took solid roots and waged a winning war against the entire world. Since then, the black communities have been dealt with the shorter end of the stick. However, high unemployment rate, often doubling that of the national rate, is not an uncommon phenomenon for African Americans. Records show that while the unemployment rate was 9.6 % during the Great Recession, blacks dallied at 16 %, almost twice again. But then, it is not all about the rate of unemployment. As already established since the beginning of the book, it is a systemic cankerworm that permeates every sector, leaving no stone unturned.

Pandemics such as <u>COVID-19</u> are excellent ways to show and assess the disparities in the systems that are otherwise overlooked. While the world is facing the small but vilifying microorganism, African Americans have worse situations on their hands. In addition to fighting the virus, they need to ensure they remain afloat and survive until the end. This, they are doing, with little or no outside assistance.

Although making up only about 13 % of the United States population, the death-rate of blacks as a result of COVID-

19 is estimated to be as high as 25 % and 33 % hospitalization. According to New York's health department, blacks are twice likely to die from the coronavirus. This is closely followed by Hispanics or Latinos, another minority group in the state. This has been discovered to have nothing to do with genetics as there is no evidence to show that blacks are more genetically susceptible to the virus than the white. Unfortunately, factors more powerful than genetics are at play here. The following factors have been identified as the reasons for these statistics.

– Disparity in the access to excellent healthcare system: Compared to their white counterparts, African Americans' access to a good medical system is low, with many living in underserved areas. Without an adequate provision in place during the log phase of the infectious curve of the disease, many blacks were undertested and under supported, often having to go extra miles to get the necessary care to ensure survival. These were compounded by the higher rates of existing underlying severe conditions such as diabetes, health conditions and limiting socioeconomic status.

– Exposure to the virus: Essential employees such as delivery personnel, cleaners, and municipal workers are often front liners, coming into contact with the virus through several means such as fomites, contaminated air, pieces of equipment, and unclean areas. Several studies show that these jobs are often taken up by members of the black community, the poor, and migrants more than the whites and educated elites. Thus, the scales of exposure become tipped towards the minority black American folks. While medical personnel struggle with inadequate provision of personal protective equipment (PPEs), many of these essential workers had to fend for themselves.

– Low socioeconomic status: The disparity in the socioeconomic statuses of whites and blacks in the United States has never been as evident as it is now. With many blacks working low-paying jobs which are not enough to cover the basic needs, affording medical insurance for an entire household would mean a dream coming true. With the toll of the virus on the economies of many nations, including the United States of America, many jobs had to go, with many of the low-wages duties getting scraped. As a result, many blacks already facing harsh states of economies became plunged into further financial depression, creating tensions and a propensity to react. The saving grace for many is the relief provided by the government in the form of a stimulus check. Meanwhile, bills are not stopping; rather, they are getting increased on a daily basis. Although the checks were a good gesture, it still is not enough to stop the harsh hardships that African Americans face.

- **Seeing is believing:** Perhaps, if many had not seen that almost nine minutes long video of the brutal treatment meted out to George Floyd, the issue would not have been taken that seriously, and pieces of evidence would have been tampered with. However, something seen and watched cannot be unseen. In a matter of seconds, the vivid cause of Floyd's death was in the hands of many, striking the hearts and speaking to the brain. Everyone got the message almost at the same time. It was barbaric and had to be stopped. Graphics and videos effectively communicate to us what text messages can't, and this is a classic example of such. With more videos surfacing, showing police brutality and systemic racism not only happening in the United States, the African American community has also realized that this is a fight to the last. It is either black lives are equal and begin to matter, or there is no stepping down.

- **Overwhelming statistics:** The statistics are glaring, showing disparity on all grounds, including health, education, crime rates, police arrests, and virtually every area. The black communities are always getting the short end of the stick because the system is programmed to do just that. More than ever before, people are aware of these facts and figures, sending the message that something has to be done or soon, it would get out of hand. The "Black Lives Matter" movement originally started as a vision championed by young blacks, but this has changed over time. The older blacks are buying into the movement and and much more. There is even a surge of young and old Caucasians abading the battle against systemic racism. The statistics have shown the connecting dots, and in turn, the way to handle it.

- **Enlightenment and education:** With the availability of the internet, web services, and several social media platforms, information is only a click away. Many people have clicked that button to get the necessary information, going as far as delving into over four hundred years history of the police. These statistics were hard to come by in past times but not any longer. Therefore, African Americans and the world are not in the dark but enlightened. With education, knowledge, and enlightenment comes the power of unimaginable magnitude. Hence, "Black Lives Matter" is going nowhere soon.

- **Other races are joining:** Everybody is realizing almost at the same time that no one should be treated as being less human. Although the movement and protest first started as a predominantly black affair, African Americans are not alone in this struggle. Hispanics and even whites have joined in stopping the systemic racism and police brutality. This alone is enough to give hope to protesters and prolong the match against discrimination as long as possible. As many nations are gradually reopening after <u>COVID-19</u>, many individuals have turned deaf ears to social distancing laws to pay tribute to George Floyd, the recent addition to an overflowing list of people murdered by police officers. Not only that, but some have also gone as far as tearing down statues and any symbol with links to slavery and its trade. While violence is not encouraged, it is a positive sign. Several videos have also emerged online, showing support in one form or the other for the actions of the protesters.

- **There is no more trust in the authorities:** The trust that people, especially those of the minority, including African Americans and Hispanics, had in the Government have been destroyed. The reason for this is not far-fetched. Several years of failed promises, implied illegality of citizenship, and continued brutality by constituted authorities have led to the high level of distrust in the people. They are faced with the realization that they have no one to turn to and have to defend themselves.

- **The results:** The results from the protests have been overwhelmingly encouraging, not only on social media platforms but from several considerations and reforms. There is a consolation when many people unconnected by many factors come together to fight a particular cause. This is the case of the Black Lives Matter. This time around, the fight is not restricted to Minneapolis, Minnesota, the place of George Floyd's death. Protests are ongoing in all of the fifty states of the United States of America and active in about three hundred and fifty cities. This is a success on a big scale. Furthermore, several other countries have witnessed protests or some sort of support for the movement decrying the death of George Floyd.

At some stage during the protest, President Trump had to be evacuated to the bunker, showing that he was not immune to the results of the protests. Also placed in the spotlight, the Minneapolis Mayor Jacob Frey could not answer the question of whether the Minneapolis department would be defunded. However, councilors have committed to dismantling the notorious police force although votes are yet to be given on the matter. In the same vein, the New York mayor Bill de Blasio promised a redirection of some the funds allotted to the New York City Police Department (NYPD) to causes concerning youths and social services. He further promised the reformation of the section-50 A which restricts public access to police officer's disciplinary records. All of these were contained in his tweets on the 7th of June 2020 as he promised not only to listen but to act as well. These considerations came after the protesters pointed out the huge fund allotted to the NYPD during a time when social service budget was being threatened. Unable to see any reason to sustain such huge amounts, the fund is set to be dispersed across other social service boards.

Many people, both ordinary citizens and influencers of varying levels and races have joined in the protests, lending the credibility of their voices. In what is considered a milestone and significant move, the Reddit co-founder of over fifteen years, Alexis Ohanian, stepped down with a plea to the Board to replace him with a black candidate. His decision came as his identification of what is happening as a father and the support for the humanization of all races. In his words, the co-founder stated that "I am doing this as a father, who needs to be able to look in the eyes of his black daughter when she asks: 'What did you do?'" In the same breath, he promised a million-dollar ($1m) to "Know your Rights Camp" with a further pledge to do more in the future.

In the world of sports, players from several countries and sport-types have started showing support for the "Black Lives Matter" by wearing jerseys customized with the slogan. They also bend one knee to show the acknowledgement of the way George Floyd got killed. These are massive supports that have not been gotten on this scale before.

These and many more are some of the factors positively driving the cause of the "Black Lives Matter" movements which have largely been peaceful.

# CHAPTER 5

# THE FEAR

F ear can be a limiting tool, breaking and destroying every form of resistance inherent in any individual. On the other hand, it can also be a powerful tool to achieve feats of unimaginable levels if rightly channeled to the right course. Sometimes, we need a douse of fear to keep us moving and at alert, but the crippling form of fear is what often keeps us enduring what should not be in the first place.

Amid the ravaging virus, the killings, the protests, and the subsequent arrests and restraints, fear is imminent. While the placards and protests decrying the systemic bias of the judicial system represent a brave front, the fear driving the entire process can't be ignored.

**The fear of living in perpetual bondage:** A typical African American that has legally earned the right to live in the country of choice lives in constant fear of always being considered a second-class citizen. Even when reforms are made to favor the colored minority, an in-depth and critical examination reveals that it is not always complete. In cases where they are, proactive measures and follow-up actions to ensure they are practiced are missing. Several years ago, many blacks thought freedom was at the door with the abolishment of the slave trade and every form of slave-related activities. But this dream was soon destroyed with the introduction of the Black Codes. The three years that followed were not any different from the slave periods. Again, a glimmer of sunlight shone through the cloudy skies when the Black Codes were deemed illegal. The African American community rejoiced at finally seeing the end of slavery and racism. Yet, this hope was shattered again by the Jim Crow Laws, which were worse than whatever they had witnessed in the times past and lasted for longer periods. Over the years, this has been the practice, and the people are starting to realize it, driving a need for action.

**The fear of uncertainty and a bleak future:** An average African American life from day to day, unsure of what the next day will yield. With the pandemic COVID-19, and many people out of jobs, the future has never appeared bleaker than it is now. Many people are living in devastating conditions of financial bankruptcy and the additional burden of ever-increasing costs and bills. More than anything, the pandemic has opened the eyes of many to the true nature of situations, exposing previously overlooked circumstances and underemphasized conditions. Is this how it will continue? That is the fear many individuals have in their hearts. Should life return to the way it was before the pandemic, or do we deserve something better? Should our children grow up to experience and suffer the same fate we have? The answer is no. We have paid the price, and the African American community has realized this.

**The fear of things going wrong:** If there is any fear in the minds of all blacks, it is that of returning to the status quo should things go south. This is backed up by the desire to create a picture of innocence and peaceful African American identity in the minds of everyone, contrary to the belief that blacks are barbaric in nature. Since the occurrence of the Greenwood massacre, blacks have been afraid to speak out, knowing that the tables are mostly turned against them. As a result, the massacre got watered-down over the history timeline. Over time, several peaceful protests have been engineered to decry brutality and injustice, but one way or the other, the fear of things going south was always present. As a result, a little glimmer of silver lining after the rain quenched many protests when a further push could have given the desired results.

**The fear that it could be anybody:** However, a different kind of fear is beginning to take roots and give people a different idea. The fear that it could have been anybody instead of Ferguson, Garner, or even Floyd. With this realization that anyone can be the next target, coupled with the harsh realities of the pandemic period and how it has always been that way, people are moved to make demands. Now, this fear is not the crippling type that has held African Americans from acting or demanding their basic rights and the rebuttal of police brutality. It is one that empowers, strengthens, and calls for action. It is a positive type of fear.

The turning point came with the pandemic COVID-19. The differences in the kinds of lifestyles of whites and blacks became glaring. Then, many people had depressing personal experiences with job loss, financial struggles, or the virus itself. One way or the other, people have been touched. The loss and anguish are not restricted only to the young or adults. It has been shared across the board, and by it, a unifying body has been made.

## THE POSITIVE SIDE OF FEAR

With this new form of fear, the blindfolds and shackles are finally coming off. As a result, the following have been achieved.

- **There is no worry about returning to status quo:** This horrible form of fear that has held many down and stopped the demands for basic things and humanly treatment is finally fading away, giving room to a new horizon and platform. African Americans have realized that there is nothing to lose if they speak out. However, there are things to forfeit if they do not. They will never know how things will turn out if no effort gets made. The coming generations will wade through the same waters or even worse conditions because their parents refused to speak out. Hence, blacks are challenging the status quo because it has become uncomfortable. They are willing to take risks.

- **A renewed confidence:** Not only have many African American suffered from a huge dent in their self-confidence over the years, but they also had almost nothing left of it. However, this period has brought in its wake a renewed form of confidence. Blacks have realized and acknowledged their lives mattered. Regardless of whatever has brought about this change, African Americans are seeing themselves in a new light. They are equals and not slaves, humans and not animals, civilized and not barbaric.

- **There is bonding and unity:** Faced by the same conditions and realizations, blacks all over the world have come together to fight a common cause. There is a silent agreement of brotherhood and solidarity caused by nothing but fear. Furthermore, people of other racial backgrounds have recognized this as well and joined the train of events. Several forms of barriers, such as language, culture, race, and personalities, are getting pulled down for new bonds to be created.

- **Clarity and focus:** For once, people are coming out with specific demands. Unlike other protests that have seen chorus recitations of a specific mantra, many persons have taken the pain to write out specific demands and requests. There is prioritization, and people know what they want and when. This is clarity. In the same vein, protesters are not backing down from this cause. There have been rescheduling of protests for fear of it getting hijacked by counter-protests and provocations, but the pace of protests has not gone down. Regardless of the various gimmicks engineered to provoke and distracts protesters, the focus has remained. The positive driving force of fear is at work here. This is not the routine protest that occurs after every black shooting before everything dies down again. This time around, many agendas are on ground to ensure that demands are met, and brutality becomes reduced to the lowest level.

- Lastly, this fear has driven many to the fountain of knowledge. As a result of saying "enough is enough," many have revisited history to find out where it all started. The "Black Lives Matter" movement will not only leave many people liberated but also enlightened.

# CHAPTER 6

# JUNETEENTH; THE TEXAS FREEDOM

---

Nothing echoes louder than the cry and call of freedom. To the one in shackles, it may remain a whisper and a waste of survival time and energy, but the ones who wield the whips of slavery, every cry, and call for freedom remains a threat to their power and control. As more and more calls echoed through the land from the cells of the enslaved, it means that the slave masters have lost the first battle; enslaving the mind of the people.

Although the people of Texas could hear the sounds and trumps of freedom in the distance South, they were yet to draw the breath of freedom. They were yet to enjoy that gentle breeze of freedom gushing in the South. Slavery has been declared illegal and all slave masters were to free their servants, but to those in Northern America, they have wielded the whip and chains for far too long that they have forgotten what a normal life meant. They have been so used to the cries of people of color responding to the lashing of whips on their skins; they have been so used to hearing the sounds of chains creaking down the hallways and the yards.

Freedom is of the mind they say; that sounds like the excuse they let you give to accept the chains they put on you. They want you to believe that even though you may be in shackles, as long as your mind thinks you are free, then, you are truly free. Maybe when you find yourself inside the walls of a prison, confined to a space with your mind free to wander from one part of the world to the other, the, you would truly understand what freedom really is. Or maybe if you lived in Galveston before June 19, 1865, you would understand that freedom of the mind with the feet and hands in chains is just another form of slavery.

Before we dive into what Juneteenth really stands for, let me clear this notion that June 19, 1865, is the official date for the end of slavery in America. The 13th Amendment by President Abraham Lincoln also known as the Emancipation Proclamation of 1863 is the date the African Americans were declared free. It is believed that the date that Juneteenth is usually celebrated as the day slavery officially came to an end in the US is wrong. The Emancipation Proclamation in 1863 declared an end to slavery in the United States. However, some slave masters in Texas refused to let their slaves know about their newly declared freedom and as such kept them for another two and a half years; another harvest. As the trump of freedom and the celebrations of freedom echoed throughout other states in the US, Texas remained in her chains and shackles responding to whips and commands.

Here is the official transcript of the 1863 Emancipation Proclamation by the President of the United States:

January 1, 1863

A Transcription By the President of the United States of America:

A Proclamation.

Whereas, on the twenty-second day of September, in the year of our Lord one thousand eight hundred and sixty-two, a proclamation was issued by the President of the United States, containing, among other things, the following, to wit:

"That on the first day of January, in the year of our Lord one thousand eight hundred and sixty-three, all persons held as slaves within any State or designated part of a State, the people whereof shall then be in rebellion against the United States, shall be then, thenceforward, and forever free; and the Executive Government of the United

States, including the military and naval authority thereof, will recognize and maintain the freedom of such persons, and will do no act or acts to repress such persons, or any of them, in any efforts they may make for their actual freedom.

"That the Executive will, on the first day of January aforesaid, by proclamation, designate the States and parts of States, if any, in which the people thereof, respectively, shall then be in rebellion against the United States; and the fact that any State, or the people thereof, shall on that day be, in good faith, represented in the Congress of the United States by members chosen thereto at elections wherein a majority of the qualified voters of such State shall have participated, shall, in the absence of strong countervailing testimony, be deemed conclusive evidence that such State, and the people thereof, are not then in rebellion against the United States."

Now, therefore I, Abraham Lincoln, President of the United States, by virtue of the power in me vested as Commander-in-Chief, of the Army and Navy of the United States in time of actual armed rebellion against the authority and government of the United States, and as a fit and necessary war measure for suppressing said rebellion, do, on this first day of January, in the year of our Lord one thousand eight hundred and sixty-three, and in accordance with my purpose so to do publicly proclaimed for the full period of one hundred days, from the day first above mentioned, order and designate as the States and parts of States wherein the people thereof respectively, are this day in rebellion against the United States, the following, to wit:

Arkansas, Texas, Louisiana, (except the Parishes of St. Bernard, Plaquemines, Jefferson, St. John, St. Charles, St. James Ascension, Assumption, Terrebonne, Lafourche, St. Mary, St. Martin, and Orleans, including the City of New Orleans) Mississippi, Alabama, Florida, Georgia, South Carolina, North Carolina, and Virginia, (except the forty-eight counties designated as West Virginia, and also the counties of Berkley, Accomac, Northampton, Elizabeth City, York, Princess Ann, and Norfolk, including the cities of Norfolk and Portsmouth[)], and which excepted parts, are for the present, left precisely as if this proclamation were not issued. And by virtue of the power, and for the purpose aforesaid, I do order and declare that all persons held as slaves within said designated States, and parts of States, are, and henceforward shall be free; and that the Executive government of the United States, including the military and naval authorities thereof, will recognize and maintain the freedom of said persons.

And I hereby enjoin upon the people so declared to be free to abstain from all violence, unless in necessary self-defence; and I recommend to them that, in all cases when allowed, they labor faithfully for reasonable wages.

And I further declare and make known, that such persons of suitable condition, will be received into the armed service of the United States to garrison forts, positions, stations, and other places, and to man vessels of all sorts in said service. And upon this act, sincerely believed to be an act of justice, warranted by the Constitution, upon military necessity, I invoke the considerate judgment of mankind, and the gracious favor of Almighty God. In witness whereof, I have hereunto set my hand and caused the seal of the United States to be affixed.

Done at the City of Washington, this first day of January, in the year of our Lord one thousand eight hundred and sixty three, and of the Independence of the United States of America the eighty-seventh.

By the President: ABRAHAM LINCOLN

**WILLIAM H. SEWARD, Secretary of State**

For some reason, the slavers of Texas did not let this information get to the slaves in Texas and did not let them walk free. Some believe that the letter never got to the slavers in Texas. They argued that the person responsible for delivering the letter containing the president's declaration never made it to Texas as the individual was attacked and killed on the road. Some other people argued that there weren't enough Union Troops to enforce the president's order in Texas.

On June 19th, 1865, Major General Gordon Granger arrived in Galveston, Texas with his Union Troops and read General Order Number 3 to the people of Galveston, Texas after declaring that the war was over. The news, like a wildfire spread throughout the state and soon, the true sounds of freedom echoed out loud in Texas. During this time, there were not less than 250,000 slaves remaining in the United States.

Here is the official text that was read to the people of Galveston on that historic day that brought about the idea practices of Juneteenth:

The people of Texas are informed that, in accordance with a proclamation from the Executive of the United States, all slaves are free. This involves an absolute equality of personal rights and rights of property, between former masters and slaves and the connection heretofore existing between them, becomes that between employer and hired labor. The Freedmen are advised to remain at their present homes and work for wages. They are informed that they will not be allowed to collect at military posts; and they will not be supported in idleness either there or elsewhere.

When you have been in a particular condition for too long, it has a way of making you accept that condition as your true reality and would tend to pass other better opportunities that may present themselves. This was exactly what happened to some of the slaves in Texas. After the Emancipation Proclamation on January 1st, 1863, slave masters reviewed the quality of living for their slaves and made it better than what it was before for them. These African American slaves thought they have gotten a good chance to life and showed gratitude to their slavers. Little did they know that they were merely eating the crumbs from the pool of opportunities the Emancipation Declaration had given them. When the announcement was later made on June 19th, 1865, a lot of these slaves had already gotten used to the seemingly newly improved working and living conditions created for them by their slavers and employers. A lot of them refused to go, instead, they tried to negotiate a better working condition with their slavers. They feared they may not have access to the things they were getting from their masters and employers. Some of the slaves even though they didn't go back to their masters, they were just in shock to be greeted by the news of their freedom. This is what happens when you are no longer in touch with what reality is.

Juneteenth celebration did not originally start as a national celebration in the United States; it was a celebration done particularly by the free slaves of Texas. But like most other holidays and celebrations, it gradually spread throughout the entire nation. The spread was necessitated by the movement of the free Texas slaves up North in search of better lives. As they moved, they carried along with them their history, stories, and experiences and also moved with them their celebrations and ways of life. Because the practice of slavery was a known reality in the world over, it was easier for other once enslaved blacks to empathize with the now free Texas slaves as they shared their stories. Other once enslaved African Americans could easily identify with their Texas brothers and accepted their Juneteenth celebration as the day they became truly free. It was difficult to find in the US any African American who didn't understand what it was like to be free again. There was nothing as beautiful as breathing the fresh air of freedom and being able to do some of the things you have always wanted to do.

Juneteenth is the oldest African American celebration in the US and represents a huge and significant part of the black lives in the country. Although it started as a celebration in Texas, today, Milwaukee and Minneapolis hold the records of the largest Juneteenth celebrations. This is a clear indication of how well the Black holiday has gained acceptance in the US. Despite the systematic racism that is boldly stamped in the system, the awareness of the black culture and the real black struggles have continued to be embraced by more and more people of color. The Juneteenth has moved from a celebration by the blacks in the US alone to a national holiday.

Juneteenth started on June 19th, 1866, a year after the Galveston declaration. The now free African Americans needed to find a way to connect with themselves and share their experiences and the joy they had when they were finally free. Some went back to Galveston to mark the celebration for the memories that Galveston held and still holds. For many African Americans, that was the day their lives truly begun. For men who were taken in chains and whips against their wills and sailed across the oceans, to be finally out of chains meant the world to them. Some of them were born on the farms of their masters, some girls and women had to deal with being raped countless times.

The pains; the horrors; the memories cannot be thrown away just like that. They had slept and dreamed of a day they would be free. They had hoped for years for freedom to finally greet them. They were pitched against their brothers, made to kill their brothers, and betray their families. Some were forced to abandon their kids and wives. These are the ones whose hands and feet forged the economy of the United States. They built the nation with their drops of blood and sweats but never got credit for it. Some of the slaves gave up the hope for freedom and just accepted what they saw as their fate. They never got to buried as they deserved, they were never honored like humans. The slave masters valued their animals more than the African Americans on their farms and serving in their houses. The slave masters gambled with the lives of their slaves and left them to rot when they fell.

For those who saw their fathers, brothers, sisters, mothers, and friends go through these things, you could imagine the feeling they had to finally be free and would no longer have to go through the horrible things they went through again.

Juneteenth throughout the US is a family-oriented celebration that pays attention to the community while also recounting the stories of the past as they concern the African Americans and their experiences in the US.

This doesn't mean it ignores the slave period in the US, it is rather, a celebration that strives to acknowledge the wrongs that were committed against the African American communities and help to bring to bear the descendants up by focusing on education and personal achievements.

When Juneteenth celebrations started, the celebrations were mere simple and small affairs that were attended by former slaves and their families. During these early periods of the celebration, a lot of cities and towns never let them have their celebrations in public spaces such as public parks. The only way they could celebrate without being harassed or have their celebration disrupted was to organize it in the form of picnics and some went ahead to barbecue in people's backyards. For those who were resident in rural areas, they were forced to have their celebrations near streams and creeks. The location wasn't so bad as they could also fish while they celebrated.

A lot of the earliest Juneteenth celebrations were held on the grounds of African American churches. As time went on, more African Americans became landowners and were able to raise money to buy lands for the celebration. Some of them went on to donate the lands that they owned just for the holiday. It was during this time that the Emancipation Park in Houston, Texas was purchased.

A lot of employers gave their employees the day off to mark the Juneteenth and join the families and friends in the celebration. There were other sets of employers who did not care about what was going on, instead they interrupted the festivities and added that their employers get back to work. Soon African American children were enrolled in public schools. This new development hindered the flow of information from parents to children. The black family lives in the black communities and the white neighborhoods became more scattered and formal education became another tool to dilute black history. Those who taught black history paid little to no attention to slave history. Schools only taught children about Lincoln's Emancipation Proclamation, but they never taught about Juneteenth and they never included the Juneteenth in the textbooks they gave to the kids. This was a direct attempt at suppressing the handing over of the knowledge of Juneteenth to the future leaders.

This singular act during that time led to a decrease in Juneteenth celebrations throughout the years. There was however a resurgence of interest in the holiday in the 1950s. This new awareness was triggered by the Rights movement of the 1950s and 1960s. During this period, many marchers wore Juneteenth buttons and went about sharing their knowledge of Juneteenth to the rest of the communities. The group which was determined to ensure that every young African American know about their history went on to organize campaigns for Juneteenth. One such was the widely attended Poor People's March in Washington D.C. in 1968. At the end of the march and discussions, those who attended and learned of the holiday went back home and shared their new knowledge of their freedom to their friends and loved ones at home.

Reverend Ralph Abernathy led the Poor Peoples' March to Washington, D.C in 1968. The essence of the march was to get people of all races, neighborhoods, brotherhoods, and economic levels to meet and show support for the poor. The march was successful as many of those who were in attendance went back home with more knowledge about black history and events in Texas. That made them returned home and revived Juneteenth celebrations. They used it as a means of educating and empowering their communities. It really worked for the African American communities. As a matter of fact, two of the largest Juneteenth celebrations taking place today came up as an aftermath of the Reverend Ralph's march. The two celebrations take place yearly in two cities in the state of Minnesota—Milwaukee, and Minneapolis. These were cities that had not previously held Juneteenth celebrations all the while it had been going on.

The white communities were never happy with the freedom that the blacks have found. They did not approve

Juneteenth as a national holiday and not even in Texas where it all started.

It wasn't until in 1980 that the Juneteenth became a Texas state holiday.

Juneteenth does not only mean a celebration of freedom, but it is also a period when African Americans look back at where they were coming from and encourage themselves to learn more about African American history. For the younger generation, Juneteenth is another opportunity to know more about the struggle that bedeviled the black race in America and has continued until the present day.

Centuries after the slavery was abolished, there still exist in the system a lot of things that must be gotten rid of as they concern racism and slavery. The fight for civil rights has always been an intricate part of black history and it remains one of the struggles of the present-day black communities. Juneteenth also serves as a reminder for that fight and at the same time, it encourages the black communities to keep fighting for civil rights. After then, some other states began to embrace Texa's Juneteenth celebration, so that Vermont in 2008 became the 29th state in the US to make Juneteenth a state-wide celebration and holiday.

Since 1866 when the first Juneteenth celebration was done in Texas, it has continued to become a national holiday and one is forced to ask if there is a future for Juneteenth in the current wake of things. It has survived over a century and has begun its walk into the second half of the second century. Does this mean that Juneteenth has come to stay in the US? The future of Juneteenth as a holiday for the black communities remained in doubts until the recent turns of events following the death of George Floyd. It is surprising to say that despite the significance of the celebration, it was never officially recognized as an independent day for the black community. One would be forced to question the value the political class and the whites placed on the celebration. Well, as should be the case, Juneteenth would hold more value only to those who can relate directly with what it represents not those who see it as a deprivation.

Juneteenth isn't just about the celebration, the festivities, and the cultures, no; it's about the day that once enslaved people became aware of their freedom and began the journey to forging their fates.

June 30, 2020, the United House unanimously gave a future to Juneteenth. The House unanimously passed a resolution recognizing June 16 as Juneteenth Independence Day – commemorating the day in 1865 when the black slaves in Texas became aware that they were truly free. This came after many people in the US called for Juneteenth to be made a paid holiday. This resolution means that Juneteenth will not only continue as a celebration for the African Americans, but it will go on to become a national holiday for all of the US.

African Americans became truly free on June 19, 1865, but the system in the United States always had an ace to grind and freedom will always be relative. The struggle for human rights will always be part of the American story. We hope that our children will not have to walk the streets of America singing the songs we sang, wearing the clothes we wore and crying for the same justice we have always cried for.

# CHAPTER 7

# EUGENICIST AND THE AFRICAN

# AMERICANS

It has always been in human nature to always find someone to blame for its woes. As a matter of fact, man would naturally blame others for his own mistake just so he can find peace within him. This is the story of African Americans and the Eugenicists in the US.

*As long as it is the law, it is right regardless of how it affects the other people*, this was the mentality that guided the eugenics movement in the US. This subtle attack at the people of color and immigrants came under the guise of improving the genetics of the people to better drive the society.

Since the coronavirus pandemic began its devastating impact on the global population, a lot of conspiracy theories have emerged linking the pandemic to the rolling out of

5G technology. Some maintained and continue to maintain that the pandemic was created to reduce the world's population, adding that it is a man-made virus created in a laboratory in Wuhan, China. The Spanish Influenza and a lot of other global or locational pandemics also received similar conjectures. While these theories may not be entirely true for the way they viewed the pandemics, the eugenics movement is different.

The word EUGENICS was first used in 1883 by the American scientist, Francis Galton. According to him, eugenics is a logical explanation of Charles Darwin's theory of Natural Selection. Like most other ideologies, the eugenics idea was first kicked against but it gradually gained root in the US. By the time it gained ground in the US, its original ideas were upheld and it soon became a national movement. Sadly, the American Eugenics movement was multi-faceted with different impacts on the socio-cultural environment of the United States. It presented itself with two major faces; a happy and promising face and then, the obvious downside of the movement. The seemingly happy face of the movement presented the promise of better baby contests to the public. It claimed to identify particularly gifted babies and in some cases even went ahead to arrange a future marriage between the babies. The contest had another face that aimed at getting what they called the "Fitter Families for Future Firesides." These contests eventually combined to become the ideologies that would drive the official eugenics movement. This was so because the contests were designed to allow for the identification of what they called the bearers of prized "germplasm." The germ plasm is the eugenicists' term for what is today known as DNA.

Over the years, a lot of historians have dived into the darker, more negative side of eugenics, revealing a lot of its hidden agendas and overall impacts on the socio-cultural climates of the US. In the US, the best way to drive a movement through time and get minimal resistance is to embed it within the law. The negative sides of the eugenics movement were successful as, like other racial movements, it successfully found its way into the law. Some of these laws were seen in the immigration restrictions that were built upon the supposed genetic superiority of some ethnic and racial groups over some other ethnic and racial groups. There was also the racial integrity laws that were enacted to prevent interracial marriage.

The eugenicists capitalized on the fact that it was expensive to take care of disabled people. Since the movement has its economic motive for most of its laws not far from the surface; the supposed idea was to create better breeding through tax cuts. Like most movements, the eugenics movement had its extreme ideologists who believed that defective newborns shouldn't be spared but should be killed at once. These were the eugenic euthanasia. They paraded the movement in the light of the mythologies of the so-called problem families — the Jukes and the Kallikaks. This became one of their major features; a story told through popular books to generations of school-age children and college students. The stories were told as parables of the generational curse heredity could in the future be transmitted in the form of criminality, poverty, mental defect, and in its general form into overall systemic moral decay.

They used the Jukes and the Kallikaks to represent the lower species of Humankind and tagged them as the products of hereditary degeneracy which was also presented in scientific lines of descent that highlighted feeblemindedness and sexual excesses. The beliefs of the eugenic propagandists were hinged on the ideologies that such characteristics could be "bred out" of the population over time if society ensured that all marriages were eugenic. As a result of this belief, marriage restriction laws were adopted to enforce their sentiment.

That was how bad it was, but if you think you have seen the worst, wait for the full eugenicist package. The most popular tool employed by the movement for cleaning up their so-called negative gene pool was the eugenic sterilization which became the most widespread and legally enforced mandate in the United States. Despite the several criticisms against the eugenics movement and the eugenic sterilization idea, the different governments in their different states went ahead to ensure that eugenic sterilization is mandatory for their perceived fight against unhealthy offsprings. Call this insanity and you won't be wrong, but the United States has been insane with extreme laws one too many times. The sad thing about its laws at the time and even some of its present laws was that they have always been targeted at a particular set of demographics.

Eugenics movement was stronger in some states in the US than it was in some other states. One of the states where the negative impacts of the movement were felt the most was the state of Indiana. In Indiana, the movement was championed by Dr. Harry Sharp, physician to the Indiana State Reformatory, and his colleague, John N. Hurty, who was a public health reformer, a seven-time secretary of the Indiana State Board of Health and a former President of the American Public Health Association. These two were responsible for proposing and driving the first eugenic sterilization law in America in 1907. Dr. Sharp was known for carrying out a lot of controversial surgeries, and for twenty years during which his ideologies and practices saw about a dozen other states signing up on the eugenics movement; with these states passing their respective eugenic laws. During these periods there were lots of legal questions that were left unanswered concerning sterilization.

Could eugenic surgery be a tool of constitutional statecraft?

It took two decades since 1907 for that question to be finally answered. Guess what; That question was answered in 1927 in the case of *Buck v. Bell.* Carrie Buck was involved in one of the major Supreme Court cases that tested a Virginia sterilization law. In *the case*, the eugenics theory that poverty, disease, and unruly sexuality could be gotten rid of through the state's mandated surgery was applied to a young Virginia woman. The family has a family history that was represented in court by the evidence captured in a pedigree that showed hereditary moral degeneracy and unlawful sex including mental defect reappearing across three different generations of her family. It is shameful to state that the result of the case was a blatant show of a direct attempt at denying people the right to life simply because some group of people perceives them as not worthy to live based on their natural flaws. Here is what Senior Justice Oliver Wendell Holmes, Jr said:

"It is better for all the world if instead of waiting to execute degenerate offspring for crime or to let them starve for their imbecility, society can prevent those who are manifestly unfit from continuing their kind. The principle that sustains compulsory vaccination is broad enough to cover cutting the Fallopian tubes. Three generations of imbeciles are enough."

What the state failed to realize at the time was that the real story of the Bucks was much more Complex as Carrie had been raped earlier on, her daughter Vivian was completely normal, and the case itself was nothing but one fraudulent case that was aimed at justifying the ideologies of the eugenics movement. However, despite the nature of the Buck's case, there were well over 65,000 surgeries in the U.S. in 32 states just within the periods of 1907 until at least 1979.

The sad part of Buck's story was that nothing was done afterward. It took the U.S. ten years after Buck's case before the last sterilization law in the United States was passed in the state of Georgia in 1937. Agitation for a sterilization law in Georgia did not follow a different pattern.

Like in a lot of other states in the U.S., agitation was centered around the cost of throwing supports behind institutionalized populations. Sterilization was sold in Georgia the same way it was sold in other states, as an important part of state budget management and a step in the walk towards achieving lower taxes. As time went on, the society began to repel and agitate more aggressively against the eugenics modus operandis but still, that didn't seem to work. During the peak of the Great Depression, a lot of civic leaders pushed hard on the government for a medical solution that would rid the state of people that were categorized as "generally defective in any way." In 1934 a 25 percent reduction in the budget appropriation that was based on reduced state revenues was announced by the Chairman of the State Board of Control for Charitable Institutions. He went on to also state that "insanity and mental deficiency appear to be rapidly increasing." Guess what his solution to the so-called rapid increase in insanity was; sterilization of course.

The Georgia law that was proposed as a solution to all the deficiencies directly targeted anyone with a "physical, mental, or nervous disease or deficiency" who might have children with similar problems. They went ahead to create a state board of eugenics which later empowered superintendents of state asylums to list out people that would pass for sterilization surgery.

Chain gang wardens were also empowered to recommend cases. The United States used everything they've got to ensure that compulsory sterilization was passed into law and accepted by the people, even when it was clear that the whole idea was just targeted at certain demographics. They used the media to escalate the acceptance of the law as it was the case when Georgia's law passed through the legislature. The media came out boldly and stated that sterilization appealed to "the common sense and reason of the people." The Georgia's bill was vetoed by the state's governor, but that didn't stop it as it reappeared again. This time there was a new governor and the bill was passed in the legislature, and signed by the new government following the 1937 legislative session.

During the time the bill was passed, about 3,300 Georgians had to endure surgery under until when it was repealled in 1974.

Between the periods of Indiana's 1907 Sterilization Statute and the Georgia's 1937 Act, not less than 30 other states enacted laws that would eventually lead to surgery for well-over 65,000 people in the US.

From the laws that were adopted by the different states in the US, it was clear that the eugenics movement was a form of population control; but a negative birth control procedure. They took a page off the Malthusian Theory of population control. If they could prevent childbirth to an extent, they would have succeeded in controlling the population. Since they cannot stop childbirth in every American of color, they had to target different demographics and use health and social behavior as cover.

The different states that adopted their laws, chose to stop childbirth in different demographics. Some states listed the "crippled, blind, degenerate, and deficient as the people who do not qualify to give birth. While some other states picked the paupers and the criminalistic. The poor people living in the state's institutions were the most likely to be sterilized in all of the 30 states.

The World War II saw a pause in the program but it continued after the war; even though it was re-appealed in 1970. Before it was re-appealed in 1970, more surgeries were performed in Georgia than any other state in the US except North Carolina. The Eugenic movement and the laws adopted by the Georgia State didn't last as long as other states in the US. In fact, the law lasted for the least period of time in Georgia. However, Georgia managed to become the fifth ranking state in the numbers of eugenic surgeries in the US. It had an average of 3,300 eugenics surgeries throughout the period the laws lasted.

In 2002 and 2007, two different markers were erected in Indiana and a resolution was passed. The resolution read:

A CONCURRENT RESOLUTION to mark the centennial of Indiana's 1907 eugenical sterilization law and to express the regret of the Senate and House of Representatives of the 115th Indiana General Assembly for Indiana's experience with eugenics.

Whereas, On April 27, 1907, Indiana enacted our nation's first eugenical sterilization law, which mandated the sterilization of persons who were physically or developmentally disabled, mentally ill, or who had committed crimes;

Whereas, The goal of the now-discredited eugenics movement was to provide a simple solution to the complex issues of physical disorders, mental illness, developmental disabilities, and changing social conditions by eliminating what the movement's supporters considered to be hereditary flaws through selective reproduction; Whereas, In the 1921 case of Smith v. Williams, the Indiana Supreme Court declared the state's 1907 law unconstitutional; Whereas, In a landmark 1927 decision, the United States Supreme Court upheld Virginia's involuntary sterilization statute in an opinion by Justice Oliver Wendell Holmes;

Whereas, Following the U.S. Supreme Court precedent, Indiana enacted a new sterilization law in 1927 authorizing the compulsory sterilization of persons living in a state institution; Whereas, Indiana involuntarily sterilized some 2,500 people, while more than 65,000 people were sterilized under similar laws in 30 other states during the same period; Whereas, Eugenics legislation devalued the sanctity of human life, placed claims of scientific benefit over human dignity, and denied the inalienable rights recognized by our Founding Fathers; Whereas, Eugenics legislation targeted the most vulnerable among us, including the poor and racial minorities, wrongly dehumanizing them under the authority of law and for the claimed purpose of public health and the good of the people; Whereas, In the past five years, several other states, including Virginia, Oregon, North Carolina, and California, have publicly repudiated their involvement in the eugenics movement; and Whereas, 2007 marks the centennial of Indiana's eugenical sterilization law, the first such law in the United States: Therefore, be it resolved by the Senate of the General Assembly of the State of Indiana, the House of Representatives concurring:

SECTION 1. That the Indiana General Assembly hereby expresses its regret over Indiana's role in the eugenics movement in this country and the injustices done under eugenic laws.

SECTION 2. That the General Assembly urges the citizens of Indiana to become familiar with the history of the eugenics movement in the belief that a more educated and enlightened population will repudiate the many laws passed in the name of eugenics and reject any such laws in the future.

About the same time as the Indiana events were taking place, Georgia State Representative Mary Margaret Oliver introduced a resolution condemning her state's involvement with eugenics. Similarly, North and South Carolina had already officially repudiated eugenics. Virginia, Oregon, and California had done so as well. A legislative statement from Georgia would put the last state to pass a sterilization law on the record renouncing eugenics.

After several court cases, there was an official eugenics apology that was written to the general public and mostly to victims of the eugenics laws. The text was introduced by Representative Oliver and it reads:

## A RESOLUTION

Expressing profound regret for Georgia´s participation in the eugenics movement in the United States and marking the centennial of eugenic sterilization in the United States, and for other purposes.

WHEREAS, in the early 20th century, a pseudo-scientific movement called eugenics gained popularity in the United States and advocated the improvement of the human race by using selective breeding to eliminate supposed hereditary flaws such as mental disability and physical deformity; and WHEREAS, in 1907, Indiana became the first state to enact a eugenics based sterilization law, mandating the sterilization of "confirmed criminals, idiots, rapists, and imbeciles"; and WHEREAS, eventually more than 30 states enacted similar compulsory sterilization laws resulting in the involuntary sterilization of more than 65,000 individuals in the United States; and WHEREAS, the Supreme Court sanctioned the practice of compulsory sterilization in an infamous 1927 decision by Justice Oliver Wendell Holmes in which the court upheld Virginia´s sterilization of a young woman in a mental health facility on the grounds that "three generations of imbeciles [were] enough"; and WHEREAS, in 1937, Georgia created a State Board of Eugenics and authorized the involuntary sterilization of Georgia´s patients in state mental health facilities, as well as Georgia inmates in state prisons and reformatories; and WHEREAS, even though Georgia was the last state to enact a sterilization law, it performed the fifth largest number of sterilizations in the nation, sterilizing approximately 3,300 of its citizens between 1937 and 1970, the year the law was repealed; and WHEREAS, more compulsory sterilizations were performed in Georgia between 1937 and 1970 than in any other state in the nation except North Carolina; and WHEREAS, in addition to compulsory sterilization, Georgia and many other states enacted eugenics related legislation that attempted to preserve "racial integrity" by banning interracial marriage; and WHEREAS, Georgia prohibited interracial marriages for 40 years, from 1927, when it enacted its antimiscegenation law, to 1967, when the Supreme Court invalidated all such laws in its landmark Loving v. Virginia decision; and WHEREAS, eugenics legislation targeted the most vulnerable populations in the United States, including the disabled, the incarcerated, the poor, the members of racial and ethnic minorities, and all others viewed as "genetically unfit" and provided a false scientific rationale for discriminatory and racist practices; and WHEREAS, despite the harm done to many thousands of Americans in the name of eugenics, the eugenics movement is largely forgotten today; and WHEREAS, in the past five years, several other states, including Virginia, Oregon, North Carolina, and California, have publicly repudiated their involvement in the eugenics movement; and WHEREAS, the year 2007 marks the centennial of eugenic sterilization in the United

States and the 70th anniversary of the passage of Georgia´s sterilization law.

NOW, THEREFORE, BE IT RESOLVED BY THE HOUSE OF REPRESENTATIVES that the members of this body express their profound regret for Georgia´s participation in the eugenics movement and the injustices done under eugenics laws, including the involuntary sterilization of Georgia citizens.

BE IT FURTHER RESOLVED that the members of this body hereby support the full education of Georgia citizens about the eugenics movement in order to ensure that a more enlightened population repudiates the intolerance and bigotry that formed the basis of American eugenics laws and rejects similar laws in the future.

BE IT FURTHER RESOLVED that the Clerk of the House of Representatives is authorized and directed to transmit an appropriate copy of this resolution to the public and the press.

It's been over a century since the eugenics movement began and it's been decades since it was abolished, however, there are still traces of its beliefs and practices evident in today's society. Some of these things exist as mere phrases and remarks, but in reality, they represent an ideology that evokes a far more negative impact on society. Some of these beliefs, practices, and remarks include:

- Looking at a couple and using such expression as "these are the type of people who should be making babies" because of some positive qualities you find in them, such as smartness, loving, and kindness. Although it is a compliment, it also means that those who do not possess these traits shouldn't bother about even getting married or making babies.

- If you have ever thought of someone who has a kid as the last person in the world who should be having a child, then, you're also showing off some of the 21st Century traits of the eugenics movement.

- If you believe that a particular person or group of persons should not be having kids because of their financial status, then, you should know that you are exhibiting the basic features of the eugenics movement.

- Believing that certain people of good morals and values should only have kids, while people who have a questionable character and who behave differently shouldn't have kids is a sign of eugenics.

- The choice of whether to have kids or not is left with the individual or individuals and should not be decided based on their health or financial dispositions or race.

# CHAPTER 8

# THE RESOLUTION

For a nation that seemed to have sold its soul to racism and other social injustices, is it ever possible to become that home of the free and the brave? Could there ever be a time in the United States when people would no longer be defined by their colors and their migratory history? The US has gone deep in these social and racial inequalities and right now all we've got is hope that all the institutes of states would come together to help put this socio-cultural cancer behind us.

There is however one question that must be addressed if we must deal with what we're faced as a nation; can we ever heal from the wounds? Is it possible that all those who have been victims of these systemic socio-cultural ills would forgive, let go, and be willing to cooperate with other members of the society, even if it means working with those who had wronged them? Well, if you look at from the perspective of the American people, I mean the common Americans taking responsibilities, then, it will never be possible. Don't think for a second that the problem of the United States is caused by the common man out there working hard to make ends meet. What we see in the lives of those who preach and practice these ills are clear reflections of what the American multilateral systems stand for. The man on the street is as good as what he believes and beliefs are learned or inferred from existing beliefs.

It's heartbreaking to see how racism as now becomes normalcy in our society.

It shouldn't have existed in the first place. Hatred is a disease of the heart. How do we fight it? How can we eradicate Racism in our society? These are some important questions to ask. You can't be happy if your neighbor is sad we were created to help each other, show love and concern for ourselves not discriminating against each other.

Fighting Racism is not a one-man job; it's a call for everybody, Young and Old, The Rich and The Poor, and The Government.

We citizens have a huge role to play!

Before you can fight systemic racism also known as institutional racism, it is important to know what it means and how it affects people of color.

## WHAT IS SYSTEMIC RACISM?

Systemic Racism also is known as Institutional Racism is a form of discrimination that normally affects people of color. Systemic racism is the differential access to the services, goods, and opportunities of society and when this becomes prominent, it becomes difficult for people of color to live peacefully and enjoy benefits provided for the society. Racism is now dominated by private corporations and public bodies. Systemic racism has now become a common practice in society.

Racial discrimination should not be normal in society. It's high time we put an end to it.

You will be surprised to be informed that systemic racism exists in schools, offices, police departments, the court system, housing, health care centers is not excluded. Survival of people of color also matters, they are citizens, they are entitled to all social benefits and should be treated with respect and love, not hatred and discrimination.

A system that reflects racism will raise people divided along lines of racial divides. Keeping that in mind, the solution to curbing these socio-cultural menaces would have to come from the system that births them.

The Laws Must Sync With The Actions Of The System: This should come in the form of criminal justice reform. There will always be a problem when we have a system where the law says one thing and the actions of the people say otherwise and the law is unable to prosecute accordingly or would turn the other way. In New York City, people of color are more likely to be arrested and prosecuted for using marijuana than the Whites. This thus begs the question if the White people in the US are governed with a different law other than the same laws with which the people of color are governed. In Massachusetts, Black people are incarcerated nearly eight times more than the White people. The law seems to be interpreted differently for the different races in the US. Throughout the US, Black people are two times more likely to get pulled over by the police and the chances to be searched are four times more for Black people. These differential treatments in the criminal justice system must be addressed.

A White ex-convict stands a higher chance of being hired by a well-paying reputable company in the US than the people of color. The US Houses must unanimously not only fix the incarceration rates but must also address the chances the people of color, especially Blacks have to forge a better life after serving a term. A lot of Black ex-cons remain largely unemployed and the majority are only able to get jobs below their educational qualifications and training.

Employers must be brought to the table to address this figure and the state must make it a criminal offense to deny any repentant ex-convict employment based on his color and criminal records he already served for. If they must be denied employment, it should be because the individual does not qualify for the job based on the job's requirement and not based on the colors of the skin.

## Education Reform

Education has remained the major vehicle for social engineering and a pivotal institution for driving equality in the system. Sadly, this institution like most other institutions have been compromised as well. Black history is only taught on the surface and a lot of truths about the people of color are not available for public knowledge. The contents of the American Educational System clearly preaches the White Supremacy theories; they are embellished subtly in the system. You will find them sprinkled at all levels of education in the US. It is obvious that the education system is bifurcated and must be addressed.

Schools are largely funded by the state and it has been noticed that schools in poor neighborhoods receive less funding than schools in rich neighborhoods. When schools are not invested in, it ultimately affects the quality of the people who pass through the school but in the short term and the long term. We must invest equally in the schools spread out in the different neighborhoods in the US. The child who drives in a luxurious car to school should not be invested in more than the child who has to take a bus to school. If we do so, we are in turn creating a cycle where the poor neighborhoods will continue to deteriorate while the rich neighborhood will keep getting better. The system must ensure there is uniformity in the quality of education received by all races in the US. In the US, schools that are located in poorer neighborhoods are usually attended by more minority students or people of color. These schools receive government funding of an overage of $1,000 less per student than rich neighborhoods.

It has also been shown that the minority races are often not exposed to same-race teachers and this goes on to affect their overall learning ability. The more same-race teachers they meet, the lesser the chances of dropping out of school. The system needs to recruit more people of color into the education system as this will also serve as a way of widening the talent pool in the education system. People of color will develop more interest when they are taught by a teacher of the same race than when taught by a white supremacist teacher. Also, employing more people of color would mean discussing a broader salary structure.

It should be noted that whatever we do not address in the educational system that our kids pass through, such would be left as a culture in the society. A lot of racial injustices can be addressed by simply addressing the education system in the US. Racism would be alien to a child who went to school where all races are treated equally. The child would grow up embracing all races as color and the chances of becoming discriminatory due to race would become very slim.

### Leveling the Playfield for Political Participation

For a country that has existed for centuries, it is surprising that we only recorded our first non-caucasian president in the last decade. This alone speaks louder what the system stands for. The question is, are we ever going to have a president from the minority race again? Well, I would want to remain optimistic and hope that we do soon. Isn't clear enough that only 10 Black lawmakers have been elected to the US Senate since its democracy? And only 153

Blacks have served in the US House of Representatives. Figures don't lie and this is one of the major reasons racism has continued to thrive in the US despite all the voices that have been given to the subject. Misrepresentation and under-representation of the people of color in politics have continued to hinder the ideology of an equal state. Voter suppression has been used as an electoral strategy for winning elections. Some states have taken actions against voter suppression and discrimination but it remains a huge part of the electoral processes in the US. In February, a House Oversight report showed evidence that Kemp was laughing at reports of voter suppression. Women, Black Americans, Asian Americans, and the Native Americans have been systematically denied several times the right to vote over the years. As a matter of fact, Stacy Abrams made a public claim in Georgia that voter suppression led to the victory of Brian Kemp.

These are some of the things that have led to continued systemic racism in the US. When the minorities are not well-represented in matters of the state, there are high chances that policies can be passed unwittingly or unknowingly that would further promote systemic racism in the US. Remember how Michigan lawmakers included a provision to exempt people who lived in counties with unemployment rates over 8.5% from the Medicaid program?

Look at the US State of Michigan and you will find that a lot of poor Black Americans are residents in urban centers with a low unemployment rate. This would have automatically benefited the White communities than the Black communities. The system operates a wide range of inequalities across space and races and there is a constant interplay of these inequalities and the policies. Most of these policies are in existence because the minorities are not adequately represented in the US policymaking processes. They have little to no voices protecting their interests in the political arena.

## Funds and Support Systems

In the US, it is easier for a White American to start a company and build it through its first, second, and third years with little to no failure than for a Black American to own a company or acquire a significant property for development. Black Americans have 27.4% poverty rates, which is the highest poverty rate among all racial groups in the US. This figure is three times more than what it is for the Whites – 9.9%. If the system would provide funds to support Black entrepreneurs, we would be looking at scaling up employment among the Blacks while reducing the poverty and unemployment ratios. All racial groups should be invested in adequately and equally. More of such opportunities as the Back Stage Capital should be introduced into the system and help Black lives grow their businesses and employ more people in their communities.

There is continued hope. Financial literacy is one of the given. Blacks must show continued support to other black businesses and become landowners.

**Racial Wealth Gap:** In terms of racial makeup there's a huge divide and the racial wealth divide recently doubled. This systemic racism is evident when you factor in the net worth of White America compared to other races.

Wealth in the United States is unequally distributed by race and particularly between Americans and the African American community. The working-class white Americans are the biggest beneficiaries of federal economic assistance programs.

African American households only have a fraction of the wealth of white American households. This means African Americans have less wealth than white Americans leaving them more economically insecure. African Americans have fewer opportunities and fewer chances to build wealth. People of color especially black households have far less to tax-advantaged forms of savings, because of the history of employment discrimination.

Also, African Americans are significantly less likely to own a house than white Americans, this means they have less access to tax and savings benefits that are attached to owning a house. People of color have fewer employment opportunities.

Employment opportunities should not be by color but rather by qualifications and services the person can render the company. There should be economic equality regardless of the color.

Did you know, according to the US Census of 1910, right after slavery, Black America owned about 20 million acres? Fast forward to the 1970s, Black land ownership plummeted to 15 million acres. Today, it's even worse Blacks collectively only own a couple of million acres of land. This is what is separating the wealthy from the poor--land ownership. Here is another interesting fact, Ted Turner by himself owns more land than Oprah Winfrey, Jay Z and Morgan Freeman combined.

The government should create even opportunities for all races to acquire and own properties for developmental purposes. The conditions should be the same for all races and the minorities should be encouraged to become entrepreneurs to also help the state challenge its unemployment and poverty ratios.

## Upskilling Programs for People of Color

A lot of companies and industries are putting in billions of dollars into upskilling their workers in order to meet up with the latest demands in the industry. These programs can be targeted at the people of color to further increase their employability and give them more chances at competing out there. A lot of people of color are ranked as low-income earners and it is often due to fewer formal credentials and expertise. Industries and corporations can come up with programs that will help improve the knowledge and credentials of these people and make them more employable.

As long as there is a huge deficit in their skils, it will always remain a reason to under-employ them and under-pay them.

Black entrepreneurs must also channel resources into helping their communities lead a better life.

# CONCLUSION

Systemic Racism, slavery, and police brutality, all revolve around a single pole which is Superiority. Your position, color, nor country should be used to exploit another human being. This time, the fight is not only about police brutality. It is about systemic racial discrimination that cuts across all tiers. This fight is about getting the basic amenities and facilities, and it has to do with getting treated like human beings that we all are. This pandemic has opened the eyes of many to these differences, and surely, life after <u>COVID-19</u> will never be the same. However, the best approach is that of peace. So, while "Black Lives Matter" movement gets stronger day-by-day, we should pursue peace and not violence. Violence makes nothing but can destroy a lot of things. Let us keep up the spirit because black lives are equal and they do matter. Be responsible for handing the knowledge of black history to your children and your children's children. Let us fight with knowledge and educate ourselves in all works of lives. As we fight, let us watch over our brothers and treat your neighbors with love and respect. Remember that we are an integral part of the United States. The goal is not to tear down the state, definitely not to tear down each other but to build a stronger and better United States of America.

It is time we work together to combat racism, for this is our nation's cry.

# ABOUT THE AUTHOR

Anthony E. Fisher is a motivational speaker, author, pilot in command, and registered nurse. He offers a vast amount of expertise and knowledge to his audience. He holds several degrees to include a BSN and MSN in nursing.

Anthony is also the author of several books, "Rising Through the Ranks: Navigating Your Next Promotion", Stacked Against the Odds and "Viral Fear: A Global Response to Covid-19 and his latest book, Unmasking America: A Nation's Cry to Racism.

He resides in Jacksonville, FL. with his lovely wife and children.

# AWARDS INCLUDE

Two Air Medals, Combat Aviation Badge, Senior Aviation Badge, Defense Service

Medal, Air Assault Badge, Meritorious Service Medal, Joint Service Commendation Medal,

Southwest Asia Service Medal w/ Bronze Service Star, Global War on Terrorism Service

Medal, Kuwait Liberation Medal, and Joint Service Commendation Medal.

To contact the author:

Email: aefisher68@gmail.com

Anthonyfisherspeaks.com

www.ingramcontent.com/pod-product-compliance
Lightning Source LLC
Chambersburg PA
CBHW021443210526
45463CB00002B/624